We must be the change we wish to see in the world.

~Gandhi

a Neighborly note

To:

From:

Everything is going to be all right

Our Information

Name _____

Address _____

Phone _____

E-Mail _____

Animal Names _____

Swapping contact information with your neighbor can help ensure the safety of your families, your pets, and your homes. Share whatever information they might need to contact you in an emergency.

Library of Congress Cataloging-in-Publication Data:

Laws, Rachel.
Neighbors: Celebrating Folks on the Block
by Rachel Laws and Patrick Picaso Santiago
ISBN 1-4196-3012-1

Booksurge Publishing, LLC.,
5341 Dorchester Road, Suite 16
North Charlston, SC 29418

Manufactured in the USA

• Practice kindness with everyone, even your enemies •

Neighbors

Celebrating Folks on the Block

written and compiled by
Rachel Celia Laws

designed and illustrated by
Patrick Picaso Santiago

Dedication

For all the groovy neighbors: you are my inspiration.

Acknowledgements

Thanks to the love of my life, David, and our family, friends, and neighbors for their love and encouragement throughout the process of developing this book.

Thanks also to Camilla Rogers, my incredibly insightful personal coach, who guided me to dream a bigger dream.

And last but not least a huge 'thank you' to Picaso for his excitement about this project and bringing this book to life on paper. Hercules! Hercules!

• Let your inner child play •

Contents

• Have courage - pass it on •

Introduction

Your neighbor's vision is as true for him as your own vision is true for you.

-Miguel de Unamuno

• All you need is love •

 # Preface

The idea for this book came to me when I started volunteering at a mediation center, where I assisted in negotiating disputes between neighbors. I was also inspired by my experiences with my own wonderful neighbors over the years; thank goodness for them.

Mediation is a tool for resolving disagreements, as an alternative to going to lawsuits. During the mediation process, the disputing parties sit down with an impartial "mediator," who helps them work out their differences.

The thing that struck me is how easily misunderstandings over relatively minor issues can escalate from simple miscommunication to all-out war. Working in mediation and watching people finally come to understand each other and resolve their differences has been very gratifying.

I've always been blessed with terrific neighbors, and I think that, deep down, everyone wants to be a good neighbor - like our neighbors and friends Maureen and Eric. When I was in kindergarten, my incredible mother, a single parent, was back in school. She had to get up and leave the house very early in the morning. I'd get myself up and walk to Maureen and Eric's house next-door. Maureen would comb my hair while Eric made us breakfast. Then, they would watch me as I walked up the long hill to school.

Our neighbors didn't get paid anything to help us; they did it out of the kindness of their hearts. They were practically part of our family and we were part of theirs. And if I was ever an inconvenience, they certainly never complained.

My current neighbor Jean is a retired women from the Midwest. Jean and I found out that we both loved gardening and cats. You can often find us in our yards discussing these things. Jerry, her husband, passed away as I was finishing this book. He wrote poetry daily and

• Conserve water •

put a copy on the branch of a rose bush between our homes. We had the fence between our properties removed so we could all enjoy the seasonal flowers in both our yards.

I could go on forever about my positive experience with neighbors, and having wonderful neighbors is something I wish for everyone. It feels good to have good neighbors, and it feels every bit as good to be a good neighbor.

My fondest hope is that this book will become a token gift from you to your own neighbor, to begin or nurture the good feelings between you. Or that you'll give it to a neighbor you're not getting along with, as a peace offering. You'd be amazed at how much a small, heartfelt gesture like this can help. If you're in this situation, give it a try!

my neighbors

 *Introduction*

We learn about neighbors before we're even old enough to remember the experience. As toddlers, most of us are curious as to who these new people are. The neighbors are, for many of us, our first contact with the world beyond our immediate families and close relatives.

When a family moves into a home, they typically think about size, location, proximity to schools and places of worship, and so on. It's impractical to look for a house based on who your future neighbors are going to be. Most of us have to rely on the luck of the draw. But when we are lucky enough to "find" nice neighbors, is it really luck, or does the closeness of living quarters help create a good neighbor experience? Why is it that some neighbors handle issues involving trees, fences, and noise better than others? What separates us or keeps us together?

There are countless children's books on getting to know the neighbors. Unfortunately, as adults, we receive a lot more information about boundaries, fence laws, and how to sue people instead of how to work and play well with others.

Fred Rogers, of Mr. Rogers' Neighborhood, was a wise and wonderful voice for getting along with our community. Now that he's gone, I ask, who's carrying the torch for being a good neighbor? How can we adults relearn our childhood lessons?

It's an anxious time in the world. Now more than ever, neighbors need to come together. Ask the people you know about their neighbors and, invariably, you'll hear about someone's horrible neighbor experiences. The tragedy is that it's all so unnecessary. Many of these problems would not even exist if people would just make a small effort to

• Love is natural in any form •

communicate. Instead, they put enormous resources into conflict. It just doesn't make sense.

My fear for our neighborhoods now is the lifestyle changes that don't provide much in the way of connection or even eye contact. Many of us pull into the driveway, park in the garage, and then go into the house without making any contact with our neighbors. If this is your situation, please consider that, even if your neighbor doesn't become your best friend, your common interest in the safety and quality of life in your new neighborhood is enough to have a good line of communication; to do "the nod" and say, "Hey, howyadoin?" Then, if you ever need to discuss anything of importance, you have that friendly contact to build upon.

Most people share a natural desire to live in a state of peace and harmony with their neighbors. It's sad, then, that so many of us have trouble communicating that a problem exists. Those who may have offended us are often not even aware that they're bothering anyone. Problems persist, emotions fester, and pretty soon, people are calling the police, going to court, or simply screaming and yelling. This book—I hope—will encourage cooler heads, and maybe even warmer feelings.

Some people live next to the same neighbors their entire lives and yet never even meet them. I heard a story once about a mother whose young children greeted a couple in the supermarket and chatted with them for a little while. When their mother asked them who these people were, the little ones explained that the couple were their neighbors, living right behind them. The parents never met this couple during their 30 years living at this property. We know people who live on the other side of the country better than those we see every day.

It's true that "it is better to give than to receive." Giving means you have something to give, and that truly is a blessing. Being aware of neighbors in need due to age, illness, or even the joy of a baby is an opportunity to give meaning to your own life by giving to your community of neighbors.

Living in and creating community is good for our health; so says lifestyle doctor Dean Ornish. Human beings are social creatures. We need contact with others. The good news for most of us is that community is as close as right next door.

This book is all about encouraging that essential sense of community. Forget about all the problems with neighbors. Too much has been written about how to sue your neighbor. This is the how-not-to-sue-your-neighbor book. So dive right in and enjoy this collection of positive, pro-neighbor thoughts and ideas. And when you find an idea you like, don't think it over, just run with it. You'll be glad you did. And so will your neighbors.

• Use solar power •

the **passion** *fruit*

A metaphor for neighbors

vines and leaves
We are all connected

• Honor your elders •

flowers
We all hold beauty
and promise

fruit and seeds
We all have something to
offer and so much to give

World peace, like community peace, does not require that
each man love his neighbor; it requires only that they live
together with mutual tolerance, submitting their disputes
to a just and peaceful settlement.

-John F. Kennedy

Neighbors

passion fruit, people...poetry

Please sit down and stay a while
we'll speak of times enchanted,
and all the statements in a smile
can start when seeds are planted

This glow is shared and spreads itself
As life itself commences
Like vines that grow however slow
And rest on picket fences

Leaves turn green and sometimes gleam
With the life that light that bestows it
The sun reflects the warm thank you's
that every creature owes it

But every speech that can reach
As far as arms extend
will then find, at certain times,
that all we have are friends

Like the fragrance of a flower
that flavors air with hope
Come what may, they seem to say
together we can cope

So understand this simple thing…
It's not so hard at all.
With none alone, it's that your home
goes far beyond your walls

They promise that through thick and thin,
and say with silent voices…
That summer winds and winds within
can't stray from proper choices

Then we'll see for what it's worth
and whether any weather
there's nothing more within the earth
like sharing laughs together

We all believe in different things
what's common are good deeds
It's all shared and written there,
In every faith and creed

Left to fate, never too late
to make your first impression
single truths can bear the fruit
that's ripened by connections

Those folks that surround us daily
with shapes of every kind
its no surprise to realize
we live on that same vine

-Patrick Picaso Santiago

Getting to Know the Folks on the Block

Most everyone has a neighbor, even if they live miles down the road. Your neighbors do not need to be your best friend, but it's great if they are. Simple consideration and civility is all that's required to coexist peacefully. You can be as private or as sociable as you like. Just say hi; it can't hurt anything. It's scary at first for some to just say "hi". It's Ok... just give it a try. This section provides some suggestions for being a good neighbor and nice thoughts about neighborliness.

• Have courage pass it on •

I want you to be concerned about your next door neighbor. Do you know your next door neighbor?

-Mother Teresa

A Short Course on Neighbors

Origin of the word "neighbor": Austro-Hungarian "neah" (near), "gabor" (farmer).

Definition of "neighbor": appropriate to the relation of neighbors; having frequent or familiar intercourse; kind, civil, social; friendly.

Synonyms for "neighbor": next to, abut, adjoin, border, bound, butt, join, meet, touch.

Synonyms for "neighborhood": area, belt, district, locality, quarter, region, tract, zone, neck of the woods, locale.

Synonyms for "neighborly": amicable, friendly warmhearted.

Webster's says the word "neighbor" comes from the Old English "neah gebur" (near dweller).

"Neighbor" From Around The World

sha'chein

隣人

jirani

vizinho

le voisin

eighbornay

puen ban

susjedi

el vecino

il vicino

鄰居

Nachbar

jiran

Nabo

hoa noho

• Fight world hunger •

kapitbahay

If the spirit moves you, please send us the word "neighbor"
in your language to: youaresoneighborly@yahoo.com

People In Your Neighborhood

Oh, who are the people in your neighborhood?
In your neighborhood?
In your neighborhood?
Say, who are the people in your neighborhood?
The people that you meet each day

Oh, the postman always brings the mail
Through rain or snow or sleet or hail
I'll work and work the whole day through
To get your letters safe to you

'Cause a postman is a person in your neighborhood
In your neighborhood
He's in your neighborhood
A postman is a person in your neighborhood
A person that you meet each day

Oh, a fireman is brave it's said
His engine is a shiny red
If there's a fire anywhere about
Well, I'll be sure to put it out

'Cause a fireman is a person in your neighborhood
In your neighborhood
He's in your neighborhood
And a postman is a person in your neighborhood

Well, they're the people that you meet
When you're walking down the street
They're the people that you meet each day

People In Your Neighborhood
By Jeff Moss
© 1969 Festival Attractions, Inc. (ASCAP) renewed 1997

• Slow down •

N-E-I-G-H-B-O-R-L-Y, by Rachel Laws

"N" is for the <u>N</u>ice things you do

"E" is for being so <u>E</u>ntertaining

"I" means <u>I</u> like you

"G" is for the <u>G</u>oodness in your heart

"H" is for keeping your house a <u>H</u>ome

"B" is for <u>B</u>eing around when someone is in need

"O" is for not <u>O</u>nly thinking of yourself

"R" is for the <u>R</u>espect you have for everyone

"L" is for <u>L</u>istening before speaking

"Y" is for <u>Y</u>ay!, you're my neighbor!

Put them all together and they spell...
"Neighborly," a word that means
the world to me!

• Turn off the TV •

Set the Stage for
Good Neighbor Relations
According To Neighbors

Introduce Yourself

Going to the mailbox, walking your dog, unloading groceries in the driveway—all of these are good opportunities to break the ice with a smile and a "hi."

Learn your neighbors' names. Offer a cordial "hello" or "good morning" when you see them. And if they don't return your greeting, don't take it personally. They might be having a bad day, or maybe it's just not their style to be friendly to people they don't know well. Your friendliness will make you feel good, and if they decide to warm up to you later, they'll already know you'll be receptive.

Keep your neighbors informed

Let your neighbors know ahead of time if you're planning a big party, building a fence, cutting down a tree, or getting a dog. Giving them a heads up allows them to let you know if your project might affect them. Plus, it lets them in on the fact that you're a considerate neighbor. Then if something you do ever bothers them, they won't feel so awkward approaching you about it; they'll already know that you're a reasonable, responsible neighbor.

Observe the Golden Rule

Treat others as you would like to be treated. Set an example by being a good neighbor yourself. For example, be considerate about the noise from vehicles, tools, stereos, basketballs, pets, and so on.

Be aware of differences

Differences in age, ethnic background, years in the neighborhood, and so on can lead to conflicting expectations and misunderstandings. That's why it's important to make an effort to communicate.

Consider your neighbors' points of view

How does your compost pile, play equipment, or car parts inventory look from the neighbors' backyards or windows? Keep areas in others' view reasonably presentable.

Be appreciative

If a neighbor does something you like, tell them! They'll be pleased to hear that you noticed their yard work or the new paint job and it will be easier to talk later if they do something you don't like.

Be positive

If your neighbor does something that irritates you, don't assume it was on purpose. Most people don't intentionally try to create problems. Give them the benefit of the doubt. Assuming that the other person is the enemy drastically reduces the probability of an amicable resolution.

• Good education for everyone •

Neighborly Philosophies

Buddhism

Full of love for all things in the world; practicing
virtue in order to benefit others, this man alone is happy.

Judge not thy neighbor.

Confucianism

Seek to be in harmony with all your neighbors; live in amity with
your brethren.

A man obtains a proper rule of action by looking on his neighbor
as himself.

Christianity

Do unto others as you would have them do unto you, for this is
the law and the prophets.

A new commandment I give to you, that you love one another;
even as I have loved you... By this all men will know that you are
my disciples; if you have love for one another.

Love does no harm to a neighbor; therefore love is fulfillment of
the law.

We're to love our neighbors as ourselves.

You shall not bear dishonest witness against your neighbor.

A man obtains a proper rule of action by looking on his neighbor
as himself.

Hinduism

This is the sum of all true righteousness… Treat others, as thou wouldst thyself be treated. Do nothing to thy neighbor, which hereafter thou wouldst not have thy neighbor do to thee.

Hindu/Bhakti Sect

Divine love could also be expressed through love of one's neighbors.

Hopi Indians

The Hopi Indians say that we all began together; that each race went on a journey to learn its own road to power, and changed; that now it is the time for us to return, to put the pieces of the puzzle back together, to make the circle whole.
— *Starhawk*

Islam

"O Messenger of Allah! I have two neighbors. To whom shall I send my gifts?" He said, "To the one whose gate is nearer to you."

Judaism

What is hurtful to yourself do not to your fellow man. This is the whole of the Torah and the remainder is but commentary.

Speak ye everyman truth to his neighbor; execute the judgment of truth and peace in your gates.

What does your religion say about being a good neighbor?
Let us know at youaresoneighborly@yahoo.com.

• No dumping •

Native American Prayer

Oh Great Spirit, grant that I may never find fault with my neighbor until I have walked the trail of life in his moccasins.

Shintoism

Regard heave as your father, each as your mother, and all things as your brothers and sisters.

It does me no injury for my neighbor to say there are twenty gods or no god.

-Thomas Jefferson

If a profound gulf separates my neighbor's belief from mine, there is always the golden bridge of tolerance.

-Anonymous Quote

His Hometown

When he was a boy sittin' in school,
Starin' out the windows at the view he knew,
All that he wanted was to be there too,
Driving his tractor through the morning dew,
Dust from the sun, mud from the rain,
Felt like an honor to him all the same,
It's the simplest thing, he's a self taught man,
He loves his work because he loves the land,

And he can change the hills, plant the trees,
Dig the wells, spread the seeds,
Mow the fields, plow the streets,
In his hometown,
And the seasons go by year into year,
He's worked all his life,
And he's worked right here,
Winters go slow if a snow storm comes,
And it's soon to be summer when the tractors hum,

I've seen him do things I just can't believe,
Makes gentle giants of those big machines,
He moves a boulder like a paper bag,
And he moves a tree like it was all he had.

And blessed is the soul who has truly found,
Something to rest on while the world turns round,
I think he'd say this is how he feels,
When the dark earth is turning underneath his wheels

Words and Music by Cheryl Wheeler
Copyright 1999
Penrod and Higgins Music/ Amachrist Music ASCAP
Used By Permission All rights reserved

Quarter Moon

And they seem to know each other very well
They speak across the garden and not a soul could tell
They can read the summer sky and they can hear the back brook swell
And they seem to know each other very well

And they drive up north on sunday afternoons
And he buys her wooden windmills and whales and quarter moons
She feeds the birds all winter and she knows them by their tunes
And they drive up north on sunday afternoons

And all summer long, they make the garden grow
Keep the green so strong
Oh, wish them well, for standing on their own

And they buried their old dog in their backyard
With a fence and plastic roses
And St. Francis standing guard
She speaks of him quite often to this day she takes it hard
And they buried their old dog in their backyard

She brings me plants and flowers all the time
And we dig the holes together she has to help with mine
When she pats the soil around them oh my god, her eyes can shine
She brings me plants and flowers all the time

And they speak about their lives as almost gone
Waiting for the sunset from an old and distant dawn
Selling off the land except the part they're living on
And they speak of their lives as almost gone

Words and Music By Cheryl Wheeler
Copyright 1999
Penrod And Higgins Music / Amachrist Music ASCAP

The Neighborhood of Make Believe

If you get to know me, you will accept me as I accept you.

-Mister Rogers

When asked why we're afraid of meeting our neighbors, Mister Rogers responded:

"Perhaps we think we won't find another human being inside that person. Perhaps we think that there may be people in this world whom I can't ever communicate with, so I will just give up before I try. How sad it is to think we should just give up on any other creature who is just like us."

Won't You Be My Neighbor

By Fred Rogers

It's a beautiful day in this neighborhood
A beautiful day for a neighbor
Would you be mine?
Could you be mine?

It's a neighborly day in this beauty wood
A neighborly day for a beauty
Would you be mine?
Could you be mine?

I've always wanted to have a neighbor just like you
I've always wanted to live in a neighborhood with you

So, let's make the most of this beautiful day
Since we're together we might as well say
Would you be mine?, could you be mine?
Won't you be my neighbor?
Won't you please, won't you please
Please won't you be my neighbor?

• Keep it real •

Security

Even if you and your neighbors are not best friends, it's a good idea for everyone to have a safe neighborhood. This section provides ideas on building security in your neighborhood with your neighbors.

Community is the only real basis of security
-Starhawk

It is your concern when your neighbor's wall is on fire.

~Horace

Keeping Your Neighborhood Safe

- Increase outdoor lighting

- Reduce blind spots: Trim your trees and hedges so you can see what's behind them. Your neighbors should be able to see your front door.

- Form a neighborhood watch program

- House-sitting: Tell your neighbors when you're going out of town. Let someone know that you'll be away and give them a number where they can reach you in case of emergency.

- Organize a safe escort service to help people get from their cars to their houses and through the community at night

- Improve police and community relations: Invite your local police to neighborhood meetings

- Hire security guards

- Create a neighborhood telephone list: Make a list of all the neighbors' phone numbers and call if you see anything unusual going on

- Screaming and yelling are good ways to alert others to trouble

- Look out for your neighbor's security; keep an eye on anything unusual.

Get to know your neighbors!

• Spend time doing what makes you feel happy •

Neighborhood Traffic Safety

- Make a difference. Slow down. Make sure you observe the 25-mile per hour speed limit.

- Talk with neighbors about traffic safety. Work together to make it happen.

- Put a "Keep Kids Alive Drive 25™" sign in your yard or a permanent sign on your street

- Ask the Police to do a traffic study in your neighborhood

- Contact your neighborhood association and local officials about posting "Keep Kids Alive Drive 25™" street signs in your neighborhood. You can also contact your city council, traffic engineer's office, and mayor's office.

- Place a "Keep Kids Alive Drive 25™" sign in your yard before school starts, after school, and on weekends when children are out playing. The sign reminds all drivers in your neighborhood to slow down for our kids' sake!

- Studies indicates that 75 percent of drivers who drive by a "Keep Kids Alive Drive 25™" yard sign slow down.

Neighborhood Watch Programs

Neighborhood watch programs have been around for more than 30 years in the United States. The neighborhood watch is a unique partnership between law enforcement and local residents to protect our communities.

The neighborhood watch concept is based on the idea that community residents are in a unique position to ensure community safety. It's not about taking the law into our own hands, but simply a willingness to become involved and donate a few hours a week to look out for suspicious activity in the neighborhood.

Neighborhood watch programs can make an enormous difference in high-crime areas and help people feel more secure, even in neighborhoods that are already relatively safe.

Check out your local Yellow Pages or the Internet for more information about Neighborhood Watch in your area.

• Open your mind •

Every man is surrounded by a neighborhood of voluntary spies.

-Jane Austen

10 Ways To Prepare for Neighborhood Emergencies

1) Identify special hazards where you live.

2) Create disaster plans for your family and your neighborhood.

3) Practice your disaster plan.

4) Build a disaster supply kit for your home and your neighborhood.

5) Prepare your children for emergencies by talking with the about what your family and neighborhood will do if disaste strikes.

6) Don't forget about seniors and others with special needs.

7) Learn CPR and first aid.

8) Eliminate hazards in your home and neighborhood.

9) Contact your local Office of Emergency or local chapter of the American Red Cross to find out how you can prepare.

10) Get involved, volunteer, and get others in your neighborhood take responsibility for disaster preparedness.

And we and our land are part of one another, so all who are living as neighbors here, human and plant and animal, are part of one another, and so cannot possibly flourish alone.

-Wendell Berry

Building Community

Being part of a community is a great feeling. Getting neighbors to join together toward a common goal can be very fulfilling. This section describes a few community building ideas and ways to make them happen.

There is no them, there is only us.
-Bill Clinton

Start A Neighborhood Project

Check with your neighbors to find out what kinds of projects they'll
support. If neighborhood groups have established goals, make
sure the project is consistent with those goals. If your neighborhood
doesn't have established goals, this might be a good first step.

- Identify skills and resources that are available in your
  neighbohood: gardeners, cooks, carpenters, sales people, artists,
  etc.

- Identify available resources from area businesses, including
  proucts and services donations, volunteers, services, technical
  assistance, and discounts

- Identify who is available to work at events

- Involve the entire neighborhood. Reach out to young people,
  seniors, and other neighbors who may not normally be involved.
  A project that meets the needs of all of your neighbors will help
  them feel part of the project and encourage them to get involved.

- Determine what resources the neighborhood can contribute to the
  project. A neighborhood's greatest resource is its residents'
  commitment and enthusiasm. Projects that include "sweat-equity"
  are the best kind.

- Identify others that can contribute to your project. Scouting troops
  may be looking for community service projects. Look into troubled-
  youth outreach programs. You could get the help you need and
  provide a positive community experience for those who need it.

• Honor labor workers •

Neighborhood Projects

- Neighborhood garage sales
- Neighborhood festivals and block parties
- Art exhibits displaying neighbor's art work
- Barbecues with the neighbors
- Ice cream socials
- Pancake breakfasts
- Annual clean-up days
- Adopt a local park
- Start a neighborhood garden
- Start a weekly produce exchange
- Establish a neighborhood computer lab
- Hold an outdoor concert or performance
- Create a neighborhood newspaper
- Set-up volunteers to visit elderly neigbors
- Form a neighbor-helping-neighbor committee to help neighbors keep up with their property maintenance
- Create a directory of names, addresses, and phone numbers and provide copies to everyone in the neighborhood
- Plant and maintain a flower bed
- Get to know the neighborhoods around you by having multi-neighborhood picnics
- As a neighborhood group, adopt a family for Christmas or other holidays
- Be sure to involve neighborhood youth.

• Remember to vote •

Start a Tool Exchange in Your Neighborhood

A tool lending program saves money on the tools most people only use once in a while. It also keeps the neighborhood well maintained and brings neighbors together in the process.

Here's how to get started:
Make a list of commonly used household tools (hammers, drills, lawn, and garden tools, etc.). Potentially dangerous tools should not be shared for liability sake. Leave some extra spaces on the sheet for additional items people have that they're willing to share.

Make copies of the list and distribute to neighbors who want to be involved. They can check off the items they're willing to share. Ask them to write down any rules for using specific tools.

Leave a space at the top of the sheet for the neighbor's name, address, and phone number.

When the sheets are filled out, make a final list of all of the tools available to borrow, and the names and phone numbers of the neighbors who own them. Hand out these sheets to everyone who has tools they're willing to lend.

This sheet should include the tool type, who owns it, and their phone number.

For example: "Hacksaw – Bob Smith, 123 Main Street, 210-555-1212."

Include the rules at the bottom of the sheet. For example, "Please return the tool by the end of the day you use it. If you break or lose a tool, or if it's stolen from you, you're responsible to replace it within three days."

If someone has computer skills and a Web site with extra space, you could even put your tool list online.

First job is to prepare the soil. The best tool for this is your neighbor's motorized garden tiller. If your neighbor does not own a garden tiller, suggest that he buy one.

-Dave Barry

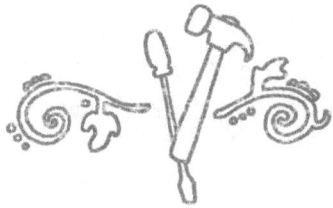

Try a Meal Exchange

A meal exchange is a great idea for saving time and money, and you always have a nutritious meal for your family. Plus, you only need to cook one night a week—great for busy lifestyles!

Here's how it works:

1. Invite a few families (five or six works well) who are interested in the idea. Talk about food requirements and preferences (e.g., vegetarian or meat eating, food allergies, and so on).

2. Each family picks one night per week to make food for the whole group.

3. Agree on times when food will be available for pick up (e.g., between six and eight o'clock).

4. Each day at the appointed time, the neighbors simply come by, pick up their portion of the day's meal, and take it home to eat with their families.

Yummy Fudgy Brownies for the Neighbors

Preheat oven to 300F.

Grease an 8x8" baking pan w/ butter or canola oil.

- 6 oz. unsweetened baking chocolate
- 1 cup butter
- 4 eggs
- 2 cups sugar
- 1 Tbl. vanilla
- 1/2 cup flour
- 1 cup semi-sweet chocolate chips
- 1 cup nuts (optional)

Melt unsweetened baking chocolate and butter together on medium-to-low heat. Stir until smooth and remove from heat.

In a separate bowl, beat the eggs and sugar. Add vanilla, semi sweet chocolate chips, and the melted butter and chocolate mixture. Blend until smooth.

Poor mixture into greased pan and sprinkle the top with nuts (if desired).

Bake for 45 minutes. Do not over bake. A toothpick inserted into the brownies should come out clean when brownies are done.

Take them over to the neighbors'. Yummy!

• Ponder contentment •

I Live in a City

I live in a city, yes I do
Made by human hands

Black hands, white hands, yellow and brown
All together built this town
Black hands, white hands, yellow and brown
All together make the wheels go round

Brown hands, yellow hands, white and black
Mined the coal and built the stack
Brown hands, yellow hands, white and black
Built the engine and laid the track

Black hands, brown hands, yellow and white
Built the buildings tall and bright
Black hands, brown hands, yellow and white
Filled them all with shining light

Black hands, white hands, brown and tan
Milled the flour and cleaned the pan
Black hands, white hands, brown and tan
The working women and the working man

How to Build Community
From the Syracuse Cultural Workers

Turn off Your TV • Leave your house • Know your neighbors
Greet people • Look up when you're walking • Plant flowers
Sit on your stoop • Use your library • Play together
Buy from local merchants • Share what you have
Honor elders • Help a lost dog • Take children to the park
Support neighborhood schools • Garden together
Pick up litter • Fix it even if you did not break it
Read stories aloud • Dance in the street
Talk to the mail carrier • Listen to the birds
Put up a swing • Help carry something heavy
Start a tradition • Seek to understand • Barter for your goods
Ask a question • Hire young people for odd jobs
Organize a block party • Bake extra and share
Ask for help when you need it • Open your shades
Sing together • Share your skills • Take back the night
Turn up the music • Turn down the music
Listen before you react to anger • Mediate a conflict
Learn new and uncomfortable angles
Know that no one is silent, though many are not heard
Work to change this

Syracruse Cultural Workers 'Tools for Change" catalog is 32 color pages of feminist, progressive, multicultural resources to help change the world and sustain activism. The Peace Caledar, Women Artists Datebook, over 100 posters on social, cultural, and political themes, holiday cards for Solstice, Christmas, Chanukah, Kwanza, plus buttons, stickers, T-shirts, notecards, post cards, and books. Great fundraising products. Box 6367, Syracruse, NY 13217 (315)474-1132; Free Fax (877)265-5399. 24 Hour ordering - Visa/MC. e-mail: scw@syrculturalworkers.org

Organizing a Babysitting Exchange

Does your neighborhood have a lot of kids? Why not organize a babysitting exchange? It's great for when people can't afford or can't find a good babysitter, especially on short notice. It's also nice for when you just need to run an errand and you don't want to bring the kids.

Organizing a neighborhood babysitting exchange is easy and fun. Just follow these simple steps:

1. Bring all the parents in your neighborhood together to talk about babysitting needs.

2. Discuss everyone's definition of "babysitting." Agree on a list of rules and responsibilities. Write it up and give everyone a copy.

3. Find out when parents are available for babysitting, and make a calendar for each month.

4. Design a one-hour "babysitting coupon" on a computer or have someone who's artistic do it by hand. Each family can start out with five hours' worth of babysitting coupons.

5. When you take your child to the neighbors for babysitting, give them coupons for the number of hours they watched your child.

6. If you're staying in on a Saturday night and several families want to go out, you can collect a lot of coupons!

• Support the arts •

A man is called selfish not for pursuing his own good, but for neglecting his neighbor's.

–Richard Whately

The duty of helping one's self in the highest sense
involves the helping of one's neighbors.
-Samuel Smiles

Start a Brain Exchange

What is a Brain Exchange?

The Brain Exchange is a brainstorming group typically for women. Affiliated "Brain Exchange" groups are forming all the time. People get together to brainstorm about relationships, in-laws, children, career, quality of life, entrepreneurial ideas, marketing strategies, titles for books they're writing, names for their babies, and more.

Brain Exchange is an opportunity to meet like-minded people to exchange support for work and personal issues, and to network. It encourages people to share their new projects, ideas, and concerns, and to explore transitions. It uses a structured process and traditional brainstorming guidelines to generate creative ideas.

Brain Exchange questions range from the deeply personal (How do I know if it's time to get out of my marriage?) to the slightly offbeat (What are some creative ways I can learn Spanish?).

Here are some questions that have been brainstormed over the years:

- How do I go about renting out a room in my house?
- What can I do with my elderly parents when they come to visit?
- How do I deal with becoming more dependent because of a chronic disease?

How to get started:

1. Find a friend to be a co-organizer (one to facilitate, one to take notes). Invite a few friends, and ask them to invite some of their friends. Explain the group's purpose and structure; that it's not therapy or a support group, but a structured environment for exchanging ideas. Ideally, you'll have 15-20 people at the first meeting. Some will come back; some won't. Don't worry, word of mouth will keep it going.

2. Set a consistent location, day of the month, and time. To keep it simple, don't request RSVPs (overflow can sit on the floor). If the usual facilitator can't make it one month, keep the same location and time and ask someone else to keep things on track. Read your defined guidelines at the beginning of each meeting. It's important to keep the structure.

3. Use a timer to control the long-winded talkers. A few minutes is plenty. When the time's up, ask the speaker to "give an action statement please." The key to success is suggestions for action, not personal stories (those can be shared during breaks).

4. At the end of the meeting, announce that it's okay to bring or send new people. Diversity breeds more varied and interesting suggestions.

5. Start on time, end on time, and enforce time limits. People can show up early or stay after if they want to socialize.

For more information please visit
www.thebrainexchange.com

• Stop polluting •

My Neighbor...

I asked some people if they ever had a neighbor who did something nice for them. Here are some of their answers:

My neighbor got together with other neighbors and cleaned up my house and yard because I'm too old to do it.

My neighbor gives me her surplus veggies.

My neighbor saved my house from burning down.

My neighbor made me Thanksgiving dinner when I had nowhere to go.

My neighbor and I garden together.

My neighbor let me know I left my car lights on.

My neighbor made me chocolate chip cookies when I really wanted some chocolate.

My neighbor found my kitty.

My neighbor was there to help plow the driveway.

• Follow your bliss •

My neighbor and I went through our refrigerators and combined ingredients to make potato pancakes.

My neighbor would come over in the mornings and pick up our new baby so my husband and I could "connect."

What neighborly experiences have you had? Let us know for future reprints of this book @ www.folksontheblock.com

having Fun together

There is nothing better than spending time in your own community and having a good time. This section describes ways in which you can do that with the neighbors.

The great renewal of the world will perhaps consist in this, that man and maid, freed of all false feelings and reluctances, will seek each other not as opposites, but as brother and sister, as neighbors, and will come together as human beings.

-Rainer Maria Rilke

Nothing makes you more tolerant of a neighbor's noisy party than being there.

-Franklin P. Jones

Throw a Block Party

Americans love to throw patio parties and backyard barbecues, but for a bash that draws in the whole neighborhood, you need a lot of room. That's how the block party was born. Neighbors close off both ends of their street, then gather in their front yards and sidewalks and in the street to share food, fun, and good company. It's a great way to tighten neighborhood bonds, and it's almost impossible not to have fun!

Make your block party an annual event, one that both kids and adults can look forward to. Your block party can coincide with a national holiday like the Fourth of July or Labor Day, or you could make your own special block party day.

Food and fun-At its most basic, a block party is simply a big barbecue or potluck picnic. You can circulate a sign-up list so everybody knows who's bringing salads, main dishes, and deserts, then just let everyone mingle, eat, drink, and talk. It's a wonderful way for neighbors to get closer, and for kids and adults to have fun together.

Special events-There are plenty of ways to make your block party special. How about live music with a band of neighborhood musicians, rented bounce houses, and popcorn machines?

Get permission first-You need to get permission before you close off city streets, so contact your department of public works or traffic department first.

• Be here now •

I'm Just A Lucky So-And-So

As I walk down the street
seems everyone I meet
gives me a friendly hello.
I guess I'm just a lucky so and so

The birds in every tree
are all so neighborly.
They sing wherever I go.
I guess I'm just a lucky so and so

If you should ask me the amount
in my bank account
I'd have to confess that I'm slippin'
but that don't worry me, confidentially
I've got a dream that's a pippin'

and when the day is through
Each night I hurry to
a home where love waits, I know.
I guess I'm just a lucky so and so

and when the day is through
Each night I hurry to
a home where love waits, I know.
I guess I'm just a lucky so and so

I'm just a lucky, lucky so and so

Words by Mack David, Music by Duke Ellington
Copyright 1945 (Renewed 1973) and Assigned to Paramount Music
Corporation and Universal-Polygram International Publishing, Inc. in the U.S.A
Rights for the world outside the U.S.A Controlled by Paramount Music
Corporation International Copyright Secured All Rights Reserved

Give a Hoot—a joke

Every evening, bird lover Tom stood in his backyard, hooting like an owl. One night, he heard an owl hoot back. For a year, the man and his feathered friend hooted back and forth. He even kept a log of the "conversation." Just as he thought he was on the verge of a breakthrough in interspecies communication, his wife had a chat with the next door neighbor. "My husband spends his nights calling out to owls," she said. "That's odd," the neighbor replied. "So does my husband."

• Use biodiesel •

Do unto yourself as your neighbors do unto themselves and look pleasant.
-George Ade

TV's "Favorite" Neighbors Quiz

Judging by popular TV sitcoms of the past 50 years, the key to creating a hit show is to give the main characters interesting neighbors!

How many neighbors can you name from these top-rated shows?

1 The Simpsons
2 The Dick van Dyke Show
3 Good Times
4 I Love Lucy
5 The Honeymooners
6 Bewitched
7 The Bob Newhart Show
8 Seinfeld
9 Everybody Loves Raymond
10 The Flintstones
11 Home Improvement
12 Mary Tyler Moore
13 The Jeffersons
14 Laverne and Shirley
15 Will and Grace
16 Living Single
17 Married With Children
18 Three's Company
19 227
20 Who's The Boss
21 Keeping Up Appearances

(Answer key in back of book)

Mrs. Pinocci's Guitar

Diane and Billy been friends forever
They go back a long time
They grew up together
She called to him
He'd written from Rome
For the whole month of August
He'd be at home

So we went to see him
At her house one evening
In the place where they'd spent all their summers as kids
We walked all around
In the small bay side town
Where his dad's called the bingo for thirty-five years
Later on that night
Under the porch light
Mrs. Pinocci brought her six string over
She said she'd been playing since she turned fifty-seven
And now I guess she's more than twenty years older

She played Yankee Doodle and we sang along with her
She passed it around and we all played a number
Neighbors and friends dropped by for a little singin'
Then later it died, no one looking to sit in
For the moon on the water
For the light from the stars
Will I thank the spirits
Whatever they are
For friendships that last
Songs from the past and
Mrs. Pinocci's guitar

And Mrs. Pinocci's guitar

• Save the redwoods •

Words and music by Cheryl Wheeler
Copyright date 1997

Dancing in the Street

Calling out around the world, are you ready for a brand new beat?
Summer's here and the time is right, for dancin' in the street,
They're dancin' in Chicago
Down in New Oreleans
Up in New York City

All we need is music, sweet music
There'll be music everywhere
There'll be swinging and swaying and records playing,
They're dancin' in the street
Oh, it doesn't matter what you wear, just as long as you are there,
So come on every guy, grab a girl, everywhere around the world.

There'll be dancin', dancin' in the street.
This is an invitation, across the nation, a chance for folks to meet
There'll be laughing singing, music swinging and dancin' in the street
All we need is music, sweet music
There'll be music everywhere
There'll be swinging, swaying, records playing,
They're dancin' in the street
Oh, it doesnt matter what you wear, just as long as you are there,
So come on every guy, grab a girl, everywhere around the world
They'll be dancin', they're dancin' in the street

This is an invitation across the nation a chance for folks to meet
There'll be lauging, singing, music swinging and dancin' in the street
Philidelphia/PA
Baltimore and DC now
Don't forget the Motor City

• Practice kindness •

The good neighbor looks beyond the external accidents and discusses those inner qualities that make all men human and therefore brothers.

-Martin Luther King

Resolving Issues

It's unrealistic to assume that you'll never have problems with your neighbors. Sometimes issues are unavoidable. If problems do come up, try to work it out without the police getting involved. This section provides ideas for working things out if and when problems arise.

When strong, be merciful, if you would have the respect, not the fear of your neighbors.
                                                    -Chilon

Ebony and Ivory

Ebony and ivory live together in perfect harmony
Side by side on my piano keyboard, oh lord, why don't we?

We all know that people are the same where ever we go
There is good and bad in Everyone,
We learn to live, we learn to give
Each other what we need to survive together alive.

Ebony and ivory live together in perfect harmony
Side by side on my piano keyboard, oh lord why don't we?

Ebony, ivory living in perfect harmony
Ebony, ivory, ooh

We all know that people are the same where ever we go
There is good and bad in everyone,
We learn to live, we learn to give
Each other what we need to survive together alive.

Ebony and ivory live together in perfect harmony
Side by side on my piano keyboard, oh lord why don't we?

Ebony, ivory living in perfect harmony

Words and Music by Paul McCartney
© 1982 MPL COMMUNICATIONS, INC.

• More love, less hate •

It will be helpful in our mutual objective to allow every man in America to look his neighbor in the face and see a man, not a color.

-Adlai E. Stevenson

Got a Dispute? Try Mediation

What is mediation?

Mediation is a process that helps people with disagreements communicate with each other and, ideally, resolve their differences.

"Mediators" are professionals trained in facilitating communication and negotiation. Mediators provide a supportive atmosphere, encouraging disputing parties to communicate productively. They help the parties sort out their issues and come up with acceptable solutions.

The mediation process involves:

- Listening without interrupting
- Sharing relevant information
- Identifying issues that need to be resolved
- Exploring options
- Testing possible solutions
- Putting decisions and agreements in writing
- Making good faith efforts to live up to agreements.

A typical mediation session lasts about two hours. The average number of sessions is between three and five, depending on participants' needs.

Benefits of mediation:

- Saves money because mediation is faster and cheaper than civil court
- Focuses on better relationships instead of legal findings
- Provides a structure for resolving future disputes more easily
- Controls flexible decision-making process—no imposed decisions

- Less stressful and traumatic than court
- Involves participants in the process, so they're less likely to breach their agreements.

To learn more about mediation in your community, look up "Mediation Services" in the yellow pages, or do an Internet search on Google.com or Yahoo.com.

Words are not as satisfactory as we should like them to be, but, like our neighbors, we have got to live with them and must make the best and not the worst of them.

-Samuel Butler

Resolve Your Own Conflict

Good conflict resolution focuses on needs, not positions. Keeping the peace in the 'hood should be a top priority, and with the proper approach, you can resolve your differences and still salvage the relationship.

Here are several tips for facilitating the discussion:
- Schedule a convenient time to talk
- Agree on a neutral place for the meeting
- Stick the facts. Steer clear of "He said, she said."
- Avoid blaming, insults, and exaggerations, all of which make it difficult to consider other viewpoints
- Listen, even if you disagree, to better focus on the issues
- Defuse hostility. Let them know you understand that they are angry or upset. Explore what's behind the emotion.
- Direct the conversation toward solutions.

Be candid
If your neighbor does something that bothers you, let them know. By communicating early and calmly, you take a step toward solving the problem. Be tolerant, but don't let a real irritation go just because it seems unimportant or hard to discuss. Your neighbors won't know that the situation bothers you unless you tell them. The longer you let it go, the worse it will get and the harder it will be to talk about.

Be respectful
Talk directly with the neighbor involved about a problem situation. Don't gossip; that only damages relationships and creates trouble.

Be calm
If a neighbor approaches you accusingly about a problem, listen carefully and thank them for letting you know how they feel. You don't have to agree or justify your behavior. If you can listen and not react defensively, their anger will subside, the lines of communication will be open, and there's a good chance of working things out.

Listen well
When you discuss a problem, try to understand how your
neighbor feels about the issue and why. Understanding, which is not
the same as agreeing, will increase the likelihood of finding a solu-
tion that works for both of you.

Take your time
Take a break to think about what you and your neighbor have dis-
cussed. Arrange to finish the conversation later, and then be sure you
do it. Starting something and not following through can make things
worse.

Communication can resolve conflict, and talking things over is the
best way to handle problems and avoid escalation. For help talking to a neighbor, or for confidential assistance with a conflict, call a
mediation center in your community.

Do not hurt your neighbor, for it is not him you wrong but yourself.
- Shawnee proverb

Virtue is not left to stand alone. He who practices it will have neighbors.

-Confucius

We forge gradually our greatest instrument for understanding the world-introspection. We discover that humanity may resemble us very considerably - that the best way of knowing the inwardness of our neighbors is to know ourselves.

-Walter Lippmann

It is a folly to punish your neighbor by fire when you live next door.

-Publilus Syrus

The love of our neighbor in all its fullness simply means being able to say to him, "What are you going through?"

-Simone Weil

The capacity for getting along with our neighbor depends to a large extent on the capacity for getting along with ourselves. The self-respecting individual will try to be as tolerant of his neighbor's shortcomings as he is of his own.

-Eric Hoffer

Each man takes care that his neighbor shall not cheat him. But a day comes when he begins to care that he does not cheat his neighbor. Then all goes well-he has changed his market-cart into a chariot of the sun.

-Ralph Waldo Emerson

Sticky

Being but one in six thousand millions
You may at times feel slightly outnumbered
America says the same using billions
Claiming they feel less encumbered

An example culturally viewed
How we differ from one another
It's only the conditioning used
We have but one earth as mother

We use these differences as brings
Made of minor cultural variations
And using only mirrors and tricks
Build walls between great nations

Seeing your neighbor build a wall
That is far beyond his real need
Creates fear and a defensive call
The big stick becomes the creed

Break this vicious cycle of sticks
Toss them onto the common fire
It is the only way to truly fix
Big Problems…small differences sire

Jeremiah Buckley
Reprinted with Permission

The best way to knock the chip off your neighbor's shoulder is to pat him on the back.

-Unknown

• Remember to listen •

The Names Of The T.U. Neighbors (answers)

1 The Flanders family
2 Millie
3 Willona Woods
4 Fred and Ethel Mertz
5 Ed and Trixie Norton
6 Abner and Gladys Kravitz
7 Howard Borden
8 Cosmo Kramer
9 Frank and Marie Barone
10 Barney and Betty Rubble
11 Wilson W. Wilson, Jr.
12 Rhoda Morgenstern, Phillis Lindstrom
13 Tom, Helen, and Allan Willis
14 Lenny Kosnowski, Andrew "Squiggy" Squiggman
15 Jack McFarland
16 Kyle Barker, Overton "Obie" Wakfield Jones
17 Steve and Marcy Rhoades-D'Arcy
18 Stanley and Helen Roper, Larry Dallas and, later, Ralph Furley
19 Rose Lee Halloway, Sandra Clark
20 Mona Robinson
21 Elizabeth and Emmet Hawksworth

What Are You Willing To Do For Your Neighbor?

If you are offering this book as a gift for your neighbor, it might be nice to let them know what types of neighborly activities you would be willing to do. Checking the boxes does not mean that you will always be available to do it, but that the intention is there.

Check the boxes next to the things you'd be willing to do for your neighbor:

- ☐ Keep an eye on your house for unusual activity and alert you to it as soon as possible

- ☐ Watch your house while you are away

- ☐ Go walking or running, play tennis, go swimming, and so on

- ☐ If I have it, lend you eggs, milk, or butter in case you forget it at the store

- ☐ Say hello when you go by

- ☐ Help organize neighborhood projects

- ☐ Share and lend tools and supplies

- ☐ Help keep peace in the neighborhood

- ☐ Call you to share information about activities in the neigborhood

- ☐ In case we have any issues or disagreements, share our concerns with one another calmly, calling the police or going to court as a last resort

  Other things we are willing to do...

  ☐
  ☐
  ☐

Notes

Notes

Notes

• Give in any way you can •

Notes

Notes

• Save the whales •

Be at war with your vices, at peace with your
neighbors, and let every new year find you a better man.

-Benjamin Franklin

www.ingramcontent.com/pod-product-compliance
Lightning Source LLC
Chambersburg PA
CBHW060436290526
45791CB00002B/961